THE BUILDINGS OF ANCIENT MESOPOTAMIA

Helen and Richard Leacroft

BROCKHAMPTON PRESS (LEICESTER) U.K.
and
YOUNG SCOTT BOOKS
Addison-Wesley Publishing Company, Inc.
Reading, Massachusetts 01867 U.S.A.

Copyright © 1974 by Helen and Richard Leacroft   All rights reserved   CIP data on last page of text

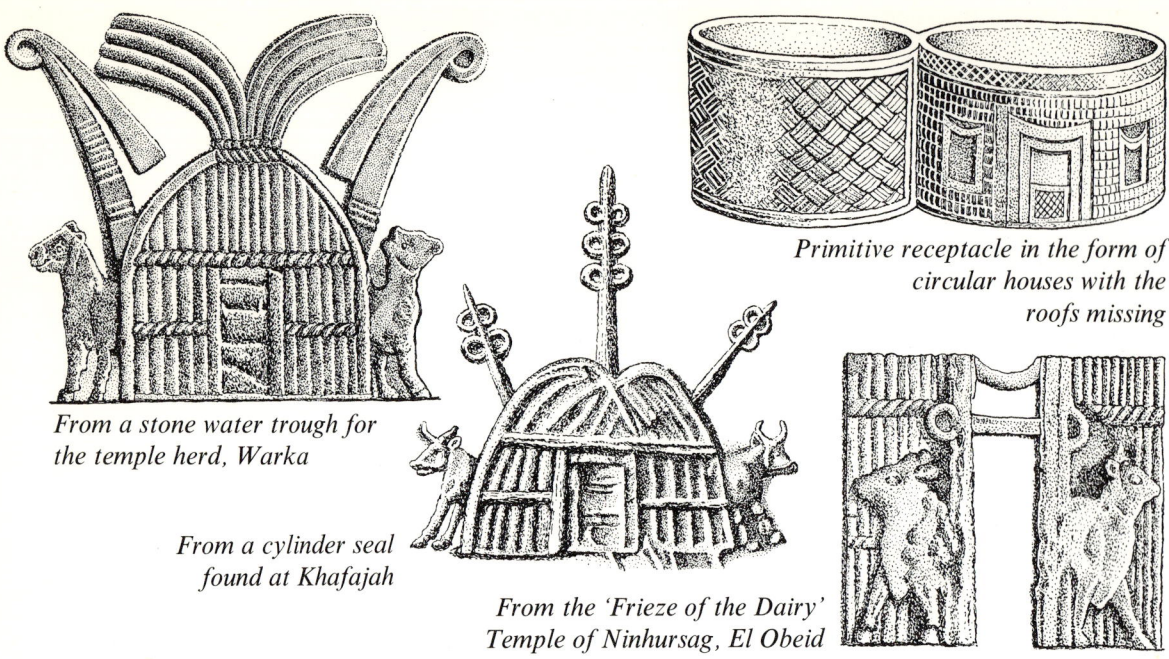

From a stone water trough for the temple herd, Warka

Primitive receptacle in the form of circular houses with the roofs missing

From a cylinder seal found at Khafajah

From the 'Frieze of the Dairy' Temple of Ninhursag, El Obeid

In the beginning, so we are told in the second chapter of the book of Genesis, man lived in the garden of Eden; a land well provided with water and good things. Many scholars have long believed that the so-called Eden was the country of Mesopotamia (page 39). It lay between the rivers Euphrates and Tigris, which rise in the mountains of Khurdistan and flow southward to the Persian Gulf. When the mountain snows melted in the spring-time the waters rose and spread out over the flat land, covering it with fertile, alluvial soil, upon which good crops could be grown. As man learnt to control the water by raising dykes and building dams and canals, so he could build cities for himself with temples, palaces and houses. Sometimes the rivers changed their courses and the land once more flooded, as we are told in the stories of Noah, and the legend of Utnapishtim and Enki, the god of the watery deep, which was found on clay tablets in the great library of King Assur-bani-pal at Nineveh. At other times man's settlements were left high and dry and, as he could no longer live in them, they were gradually covered by the drifting sand.

Today most of ancient Mesopotamia is in modern Iraq, and archaeologists from many countries have excavated the tells *or great mounds which stand high, under the fierce heat of the sun, against a flat desert landscape. They have brought back to the light of day the cities, temples, tombs and treasures of the peoples who lived in 'Eden'.*

Sheikh's Mudhif; Marsh Arabs' reed-built guest house

NINEVEH, *Palace of Assurbanipal 668–627 B.C. Tent of Assyrian officer*

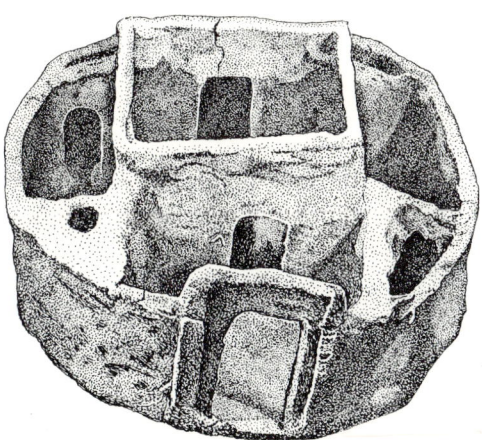
MARI, *Model of Headman's house*

Primitive houses

The dwellings of men who lived six to seven thousand years ago have, of course, vanished, but it is possible to tell what they were like from carvings, friezes, vases and models. An important source of information about Mesopotamia has been the many baked clay and steatite stamp and cylinder seals which have been found; these had designs engraved on them and were rolled on wet clay tablets to serve as signatures.

Use was always made of readily available materials, and in the south of the country, called Sumer in early times, there was a plentiful supply of reeds growing by the rivers. Bundles of these were set into the ground with further bundles lashed across their tops to make a firm framework, while shorter bundles were used as frames for openings. The spaces were infilled with woven reed matting held in place at intervals by horizontal bands of twisted reeds. A mat, which could be rolled up when necessary, served as a door, or perhaps a skin curtain was used. In the illustration of the cattle byre (page 2) two projecting rings can be seen on either side of the door which may well have held a pole for a curtain. Wandering tribesmen carried tents which could be set up easily when pastures were reached.

TEMPLE OF TEPE GAWRA, *c.* 3500 B.C. When the people started to live together in communities they set up self-governing cities under the protection of a god. Authority within the city was given to one man called the *Ensi*, elected by the adult freemen of the community. This 'Assembly' had power to remove the *Ensi* if he did not carry out his work properly. His duties were to act as steward for the god and administer the city. He was therefore both ruler and priest.

The city's most important building was the god's home or temple. A cylinder seal found at Ur shows the god sitting on a throne; in his hand is a measuring stick which he holds against a brick held by a servant, to make sure that it is of the required size for use in the temple construction. It was thought that the god concerned himself with the actual building of his house. Parts of the city belonged to the god, and the surrounding areas formed his estates. Many officials were re-

quired to organize the temple affairs, such as guardians of the gates, cooks to supervise the preparation of food and drink for the god and his priests, armourers, musicians, shepherds and storekeepers.

Every citizen was required to contribute towards the upkeep of the temple. The contributions were in the form of grain, fish, milk, cattle, sheep and goats. They were used in the god's ceremonial meals and also as payments to the priests and officials, and were exchanged for imported goods such as metals and timber. So trade was related to the temple, with the result that vast complexes had to be built.

In the illustration the people may be seen bringing their offerings; the important men wear garments made of tufted sheep tails. The scribes sit in the shade of the building writing in wedge-shaped – cuneiform – characters on wet clay, which when baked became permanent records. Clay folded around the tablets made an 'envelope'.

TELL UQAIR, Painted Temple c. 3500 B.C.

Early temples of Sumer

To build their temples the people used the plentiful supply of mud to make mud bricks (page 20), which were either dried in the sun or, to make them more permanent, baked hard in kilns. Where it was necessary to waterproof a level or a drain, bitumen was spread. This was the slime spoken of in the Bible as welling up out of the ground.

As the shrine was the reason for and the heart of the community life, it was, at first, built on a low platform – *parraku* – approached by steps. This meant that it not only dominated the surrounding areas but was also raised above flood levels. Once ground had been sanctified to a god it remained holy; therefore if a temple was destroyed for any reason the remains were levelled off to make a firm base for a new building on the same site (page 10). At Tepe Gawra (pages 4–5) many temples have been excavated, built one on top of the other. This discovery led archaeologists to examine

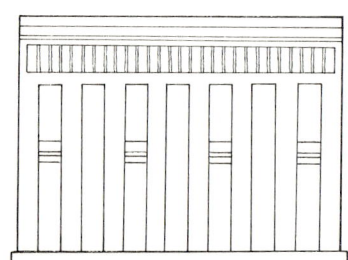

BUILDING TYPES illustrated on Mesopotamian cylinder seals

the temple of Enki at Eridu, which had been an ancient and important place of worship; beneath a high platform, on which stood a temple and *ziggurat*, they found a further seventeen temples, the earliest being a small shrine built directly on clean sand. Each later temple was built on a brick platform which was heightened and widened to hide the building below; often, however, the foundations of one temple cut through those of a lower one, so making a puzzle for the archaeologists. The high platform topped with a *ziggurat*, called by the Sumerians 'the Mountain', may well have been an attempt on their part to re-create the conditions of the hilly country from which they originally came.

The use of mud brick dictated the form of the building itself. In early times the reed construction (pages 2–3) was adapted to the use of mud brick, in much the same way as was found in Egypt at Sakkara, where the brickwork of royal tombs imitated in form and by painting the buildings of reed bundles and matting (see *The Buildings of Ancient Egypt*, page 3). Walls had recesses or setbacks and were strengthened by the use of buttresses,

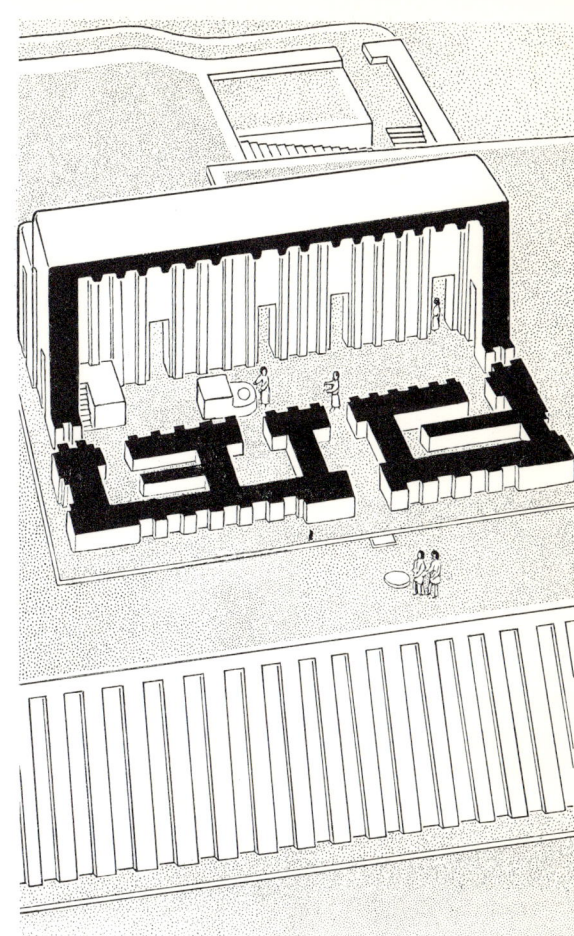

URUK, The White Temple, c. 3200–3100 B.C.

which not only threw shadows to break the monotony of blank surfaces but could also have served as supports for roof beams. As it was difficult to carve on the surface, decoration was often in the form of painting or panels inlaid with shell or limestone carved in relief. Cones (pages 4, 5 and 20) were also used, each cone being shaped to a point at one end, flattened at the head and set into bitumen.

ERIDU, The Temples of Enki, from the small chapel XVII, c. 4500 B.C. to temple VI, c. 3900 B.C. and temple I, c. 2900 B.C. The whole complex partly covered by the Ziggurat of Ur-Nammu, c. 2100 B.C.

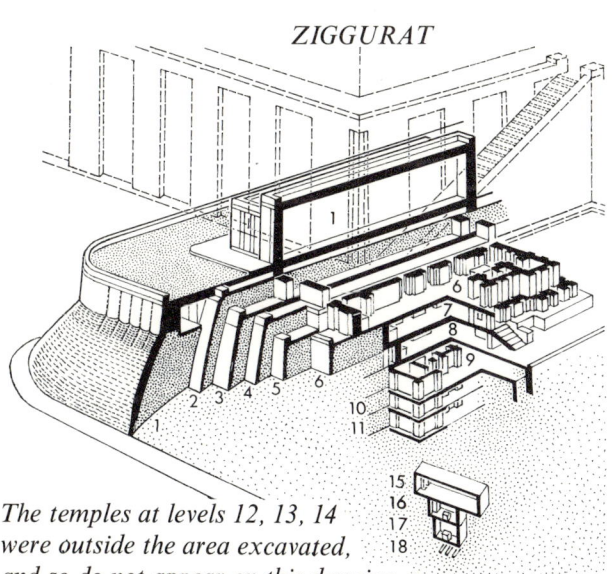

ZIGGURAT

The temples at levels 12, 13, 14 were outside the area excavated, and so do not appear on this drawing

THE PILLARED HALL AT WARKA (ancient URUK), *c.* 3000 B.C. An example of cone decoration may be seen in the illustration above. Used here not only to hide the brickwork but also to give the surface a weatherproofing. The terracotta – baked clay – cones, some four inches in length, had their heads dipped in colour so that when inserted into the wall surface they created a brilliant mosaic pattern. Another method of mosaic decoration was to be found in the temple at El Obeid, where two wooden columns were excavated which had been coated in bitumen into which small squares and triangles of red sandstone, black paste and mother-of-pearl had been inserted; a loop of copper wire on the back of each tessera or piece of mosaic held it in position. Here, also, a decorative feature was the use of artificial flowers (page 20), made of baked clay with petals of white limestone, red sandstone and black paste arranged in a regular pattern. The flowers

were also held in place by copper wires fastened back into the walls.

The plans of the temples followed simple lines (page 7). The entrance to the shrine was in the long wall; against the short wall was an altar with an offering table of mud brick in front of it, and sometimes a small hearth where sacrifices were made. At the opposite end was a niche and a low platform for the appearances of the god. Around the shrines were rooms for the priests, and store houses for the goods and treasures of the gods, whose statues represented them in human form, as they were thought to live a life fulfilling human needs. As the Sumerians wished to live with the gods, it became the custom for a man to have a small image of himself made which was set up within the shrine. When it was considered necessary to rebuild the temple, these 'worshippers' and the other treasures of the god were buried within the remains of the old temple.

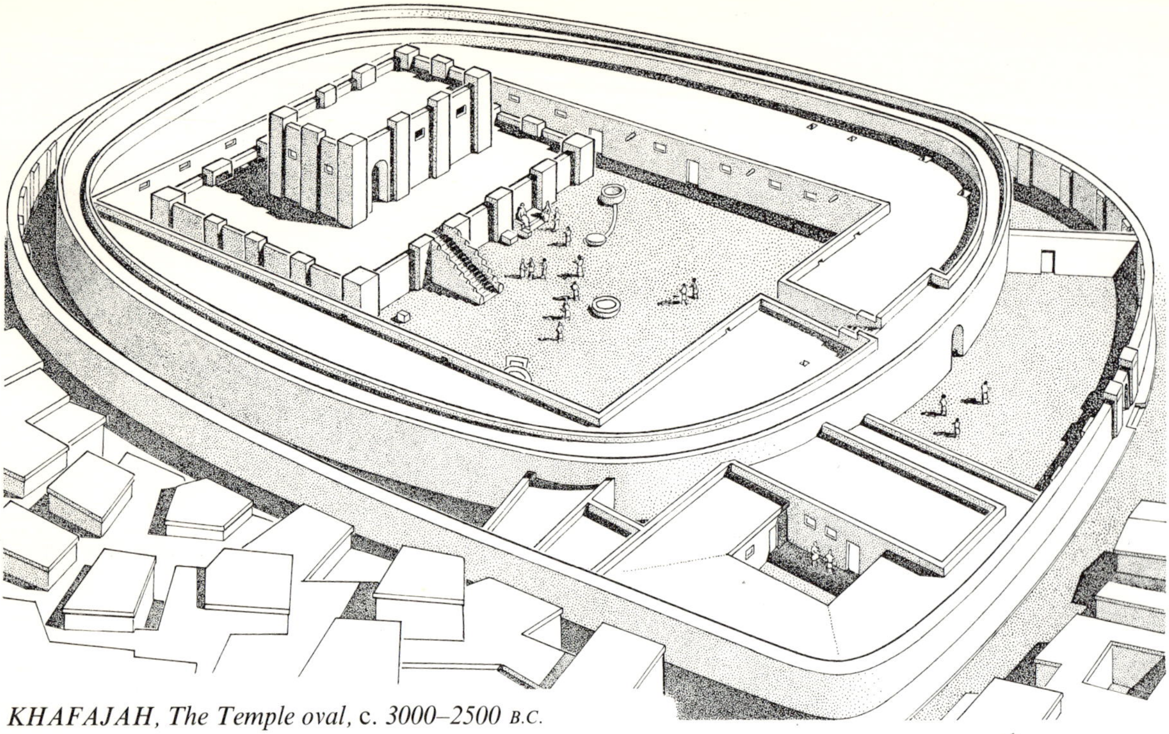

KHAFAJAH, The Temple oval, c. *3000–2500* B.C.

By about 2600 B.C. a change was taking place in temple building. Up to this time the temple had looked outwards over the city, but when it was surrounded by buildings, expansion was difficult; in addition, the temple itself was turning inwards, being built around a courtyard, so shutting the god and the sacred cult away from the people. This development may be seen in the illustrations of the Abu Temple at Tell Asmar.

Built of oblong sun-dried mud bricks, the earliest shrine 'A' was irregular in shape, hemmed in by other buildings. It had a single sanctuary with an antechamber through which the worshippers had to pass. The Archaic shrine 'B' was erected over the first shrine and had an irregularly shaped courtyard, in which archaeologists found two circular mud-brick column bases. Entrance to the sanctuary was through a narrow antechamber. A small room which could only be entered from beside the altar was probably used by the priests. The square temple 'C' had what was to become a typical arrangement of rooms around a square courtyard, and here the use of plano-convex bricks (page 20) was to be found.

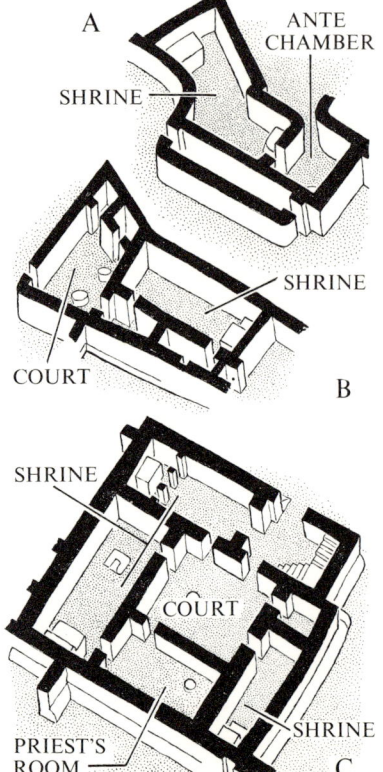

TELL ASMAR, Abu Temple. A: Earliest shrine, c. *3000* B.C. *B: Archaic shrine 1,* c. *2800* B.C. *C: Square temple,* c. *2700–2600* B.C.

At Khafajah (left) the temple was built within an oval; it is not really known why this shape was used, but it may have had religious significance. Here also, a new method of building the foundations was adopted. The ground was dug out to a depth of about eight feet and filled with clean white sand brought from the desert; the foundations were then built up so that they rose from within the earth with foundation pegs and nails (page 20) set at the four main points of the compass. Many such pegs have been found, and the inscriptions on them have served to identify the buildings. To further separate the temple from the city a second thick wall – *kisu* – was built around the foundation walls. A great stairway from the courtyard led to a higher platform on which the shrine was situated.

The *ziggurat* at Ur was the work of Ur-Nammu, ruler from 2124 to 2107 B.C. This king had led a successful revolt against the king of Erech and then set about creating a beautiful city which was dominated by the temple dedicated to the moon god Nannar. The bricks used were stamped with Ur-Nammu's name, but it is probable that the building was finished by his son. The book of Genesis describes the Tower of Babel as being built 'to reach to heaven' and similarly the *ziggurat* of Ur had three high platforms on which trees were planted to make pleasant groves.

UR. The Ziggurat of Ur-Nammu, c. *2100* B.C.

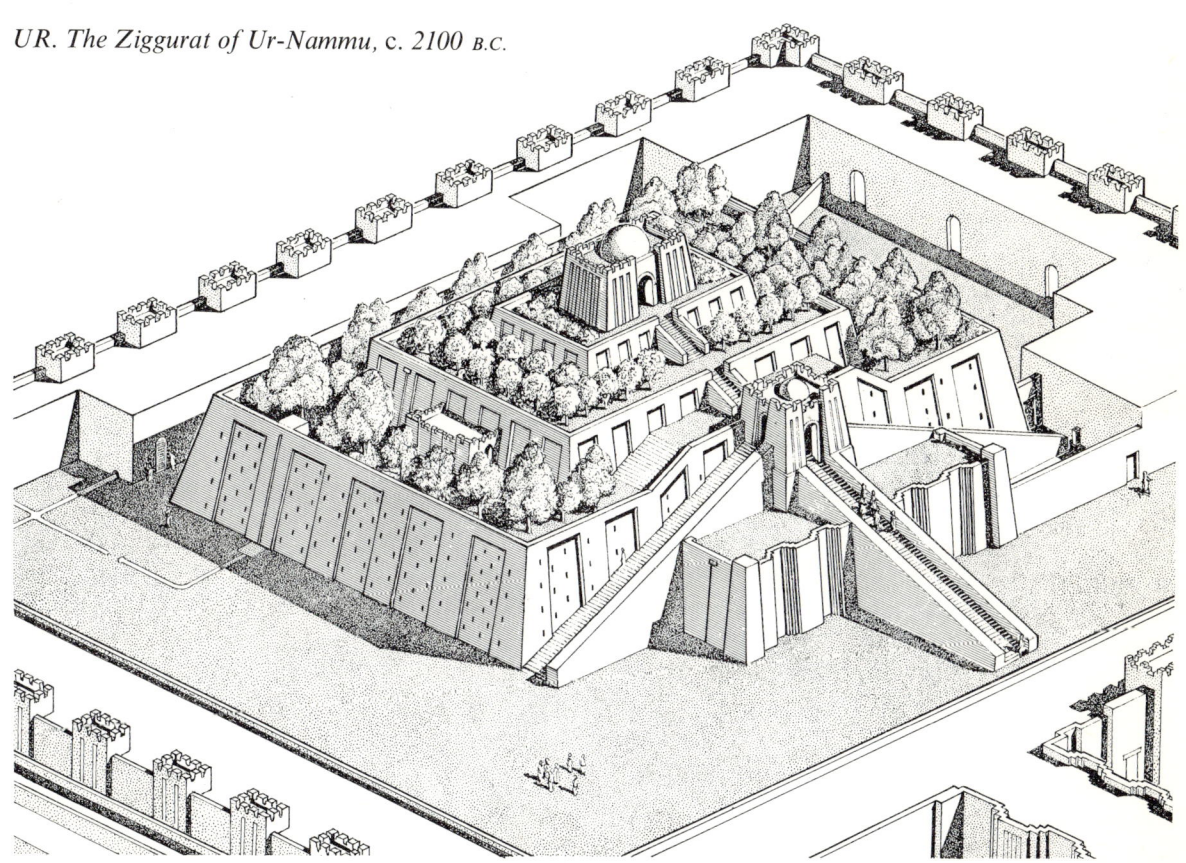

BUILDING THE TOWER OF BABEL. No chambers or tombs were to be found within the mud-brick core of the great *ziggurats*. The terrace platforms were solidly constructed, each core being surrounded by a thick outer casing of baked brick set in bitumen. To break the monotony of the rising walls, recesses and panels were constructed upon which the sunlight played and threw shadows. In addition the walls were battered; that is, they were thicker at the bottom than at the top, and their outer faces sloped inward as they rose. This gave a stability which upright walls would not have had.

The walls were given a slight curve which helped to prevent a feeling of weakness when viewed along their length. The corner panels were made narrower to give a feeling of greater strength and stability.

The terrace pavements consisted of courses of burnt brick set in, and thickly coated with bitumen. In some *ziggurats* mats and ropes

of plaited reeds were inlaid to help bind the structure together. Mention has already been made of trees, and these were planted in holes left unpaved and filled in with soil. To allow the water, which the plants required, to drain away, a series of rectangular slits – weepers – were left in the wall faces; these did not penetrate into the brick core. A hoist was required to raise the water, and the remains of such a machine were found at Ur.

The lowest platform was painted black with bitumen, the second level red, and the highest one on which the shrine stood blue; these colours were associated with religious beliefs.

The hard building work was carried out by slaves who were either prisoners of war or freemen who, running into debt, had sold themselves and sometimes their families to pay their dues. Unlike modern builders they had only simple tools, and the raising of the great structures depended mainly upon the muscle power of men and donkeys.

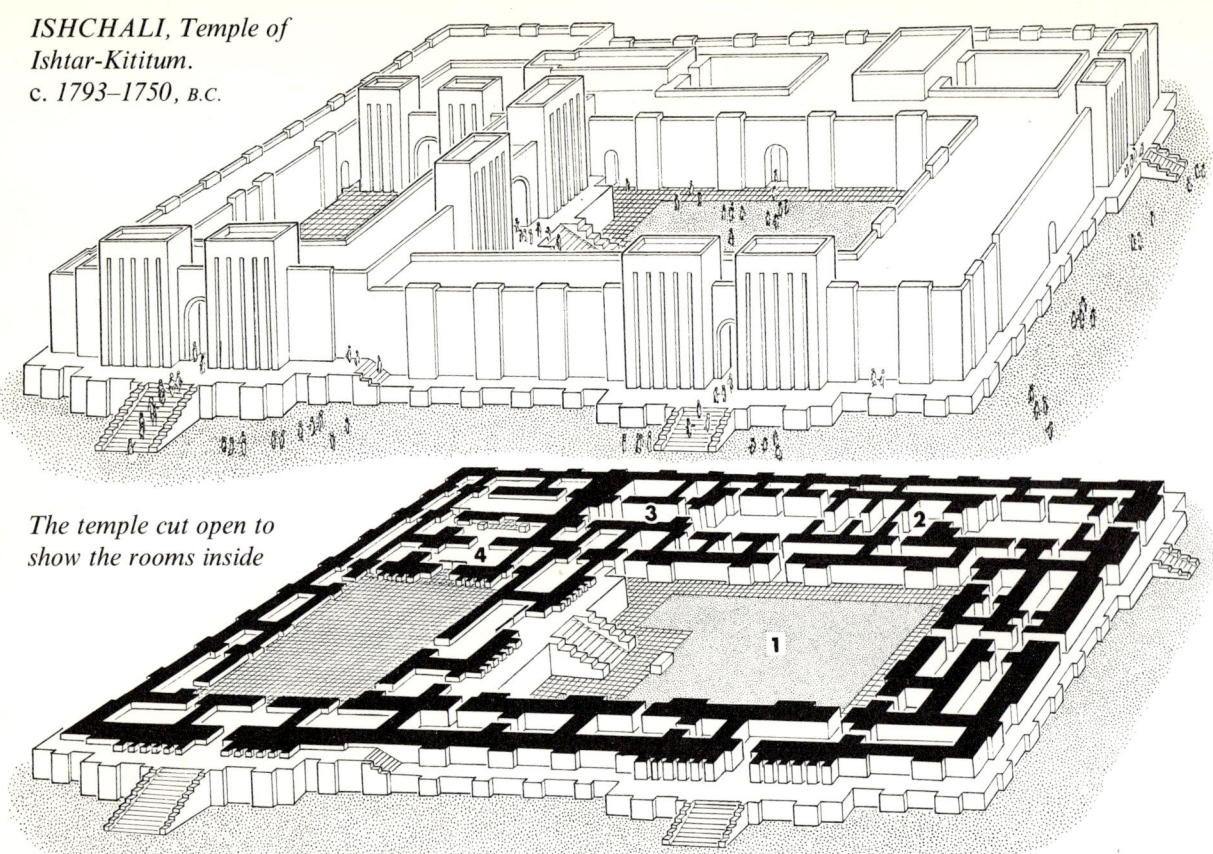

ISCHALI, Temple of Ishtar-Kititum.
c. 1793–1750, B.C.

The temple cut open to show the rooms inside

BABYLONIAN TEMPLES

The kingdom of Ur was overthrown by enemies about 2006 B.C., and for a time Mesopotamia was under the control of the lords and gods of the city of Mari (page 19). At an earlier time the lords of Lagash on the Tigris had been the dominating influence over Sumer, and it was not until Hammurabi became king, about 1793 B.C., and set up his capital in Babylon that the country as a whole came under the power of a strong, peace-loving ruler. In honour of his goddess Ishtar-Ianna he built a temple at Ishchali. The building was set on a platform of baked brick laid in bitumen, which not only stopped flood-water reaching the temple, but also prevented the building from sinking and cracking when water was absorbed by the subsoil. A large gateway led into a vast courtyard (1), around which were the usual offices, stores, rooms for the priests and three sanctuaries (2,3). The sanctuary of Ishtar (4) was the largest and was approached either from the courtyard, or directly from the street through a gateway built on the same axis as the shrine, which was divided into forecourt, ante-cella and cella. The statue of the goddess stood in a niche in the back wall. This arrangement was to become the basic plan for most of the Babylonian temples, as may be seen in the Innin temple and the temple of Ningal at Ur. These two buildings were built when Mesopotamia was under the domination of the Kassites, warriors who came from the mountains of Khurdistan about 1600 B.C. The Innin temple had bastions at each corner and was freestanding, so that people could walk all round it, and see the dado of moulded terracotta bricks which showed gods and goddesses, each holding a vase from which water, represented by wavy lines, fell. This low-relief dado was not merely decoration, but formed an essential part of the construction of the building. When the Ningal temple at Ur was rebuilt a small dome covered the cella.

In contrast, the Ishtar temple at Assur in the north, built by Tukulti-Ninurta, 1244–1208 B.C., had an entrance in the long wall; the statue of the goddess was set at a right angle, or on a bent axis, to the entrance and was therefore hidden from the sight of approaching worshippers. This arrangement was similar to the early temples of the Sumerians (page 7).

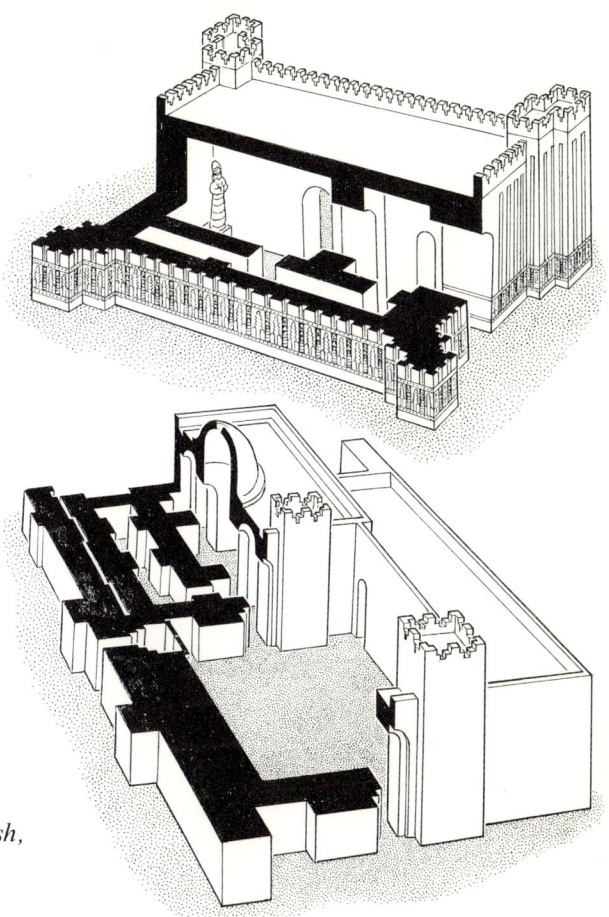

Top: URUK, Innin Temple of Karaindash, c. 1420 B.C. Right: UR, Ningal Temple of Kurigalzu I, c. 1400 B.C.

ASSUR. Ishtar temple of Tukulti-Ninurta I, 1244–1208 B.C.

PALACES

By 1900 B.C., the kingdom of Assyria was emerging. It lay in the north-east of the country between the Tigris and the foothills of Khurdistan. The Assyrians were a warlike people, and by the time that Assurnasirpal II, 883–859 B.C., came to the throne, had established a great empire. At Nimrud, Assurnasirpal built a magnificent palace, and a reconstruction of the great hall or throne room may be seen above.

The Assyrians used alabaster and limestone from the mountains. Their palace walls were lined at ground-level with upright slabs – orthostats – fastened to the mud brick by iron cramps. These were carved in relief and told stories of the victories and achievements of their kings. They also depicted hunting expeditions and religious ceremonies in which the Tree of Life was shown with the king who was surrounded by winged genies – human and eagle-headed figures.

Each carried a small bucket and a cone or sprinkler; these symbols appeared so often in Assyrian carvings that they were probably connected with their religious beliefs. As the reliefs ran over from one slab to another they must have been carved after they had been put into position. Above the carvings the walls were mud-plastered and painted with further scenes and bands of decoration. Light entered through small openings near the roof, which was supported by painted wood beams.

The throne was at the east end of the room on a stepped platform of burnt brick.

The palace was divided into two sections each with its own courtyard; the *bitanu* – the king's residence and audience room, and the *babanu* – the quarters for the officials. The magnificence of the palace may be imagined from an inscription Assurnasirpal had carved. It stated 69,374 people were entertained, and 2,200 oxen, 16,000 sheep, 10,000 skins of wine and 10,000 barrels of beer were consumed.

TELL ASMAR, Temple of Gimilsin – King of Ur – and
Palace or Seat of Government of Eshnunna
in the time of Illushuilia, c. 2317 – 2283 B.C.
A: Temple. 1, Sanctuary. 2, Altar.
B: Palace. 3, Great Hall.
4, Throne room. 5, Courtyard.
6, Private suite. 7, Ablutions.
C: Palace Chapel. 8, Court.
9, Ante-sanctuary (cella).
10, Sanctuary (cella).
11, Toilet.

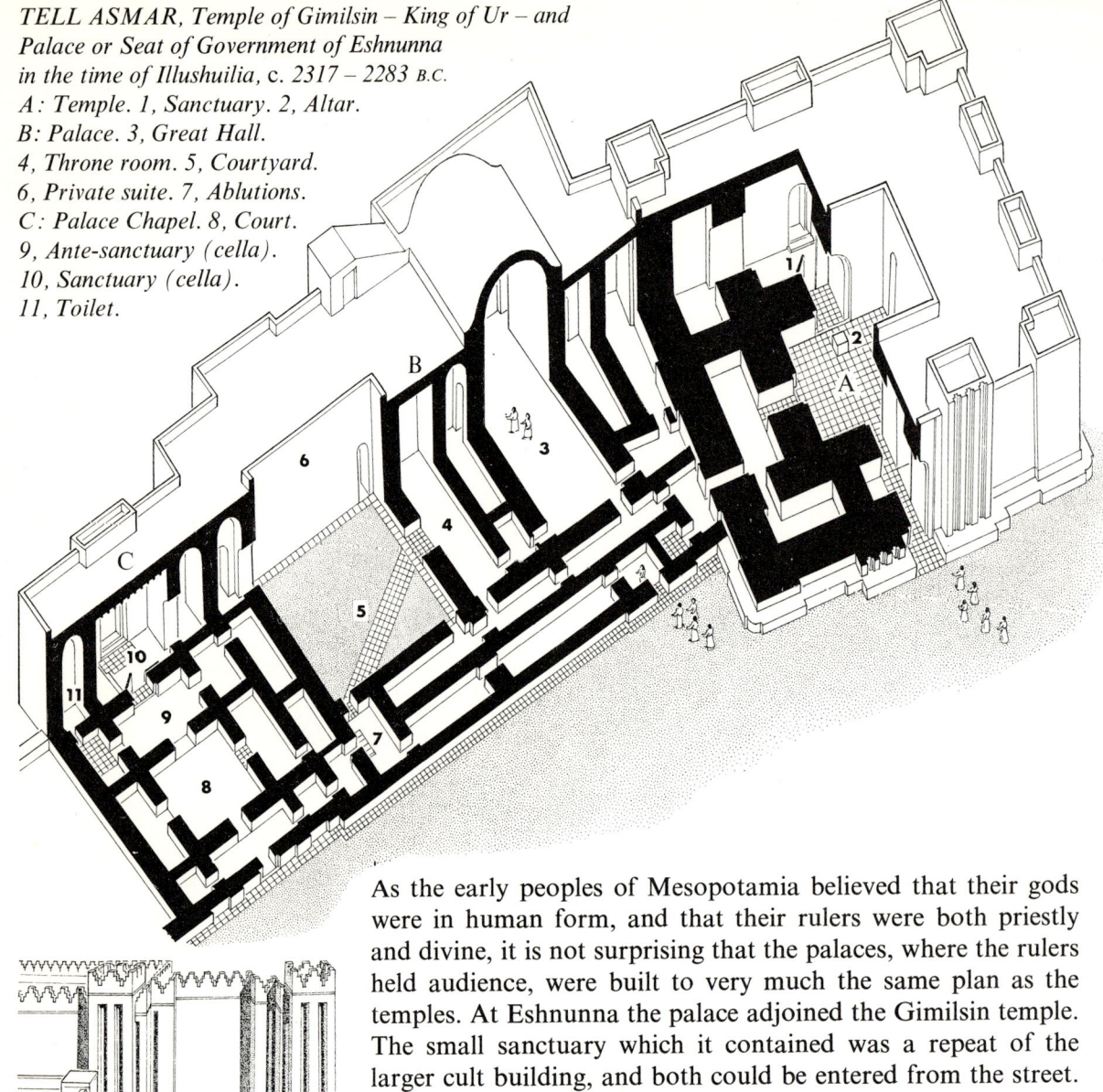

As the early peoples of Mesopotamia believed that their gods were in human form, and that their rulers were both priestly and divine, it is not surprising that the palaces, where the rulers held audience, were built to very much the same plan as the temples. At Eshnunna the palace adjoined the Gimilsin temple. The small sanctuary which it contained was a repeat of the larger cult building, and both could be entered from the street. The palace, in contrast, could only be entered through one well-guarded gateway leading into a small vestibule and dark corridor down which all visitors had to pass. Across the courtyard (5) was a diagonal pathway of baked brick which led to the throne room and state offices. The ruler's private quarters were on the opposite side of the court (6). At the entrance there was a place for washing which was probably used by visitors.

KISH, Entrance Gateway to earliest fortified Palace,
c. 2700 B.C. with colonnaded later addition on left

One of the earliest palaces to have been excavated was at Mari. It was surrounded by a great mud-brick wall set on stone foundations, and had towers to reinforce it. In the open courtyard three curved steps led up to an audience chamber. Important dignitaries were taken to an inner court (see right), where the floor was of white plaster and the walls were covered with frescoes (1). To protect the paintings, light canopies resting on wooden poles were erected. Beyond the courtyard was a long room (3) where a statue of a goddess was to be found, and behind this was the throne room (2).

In 717 B.C. Sargon II decided to build a new city at Dur-Sharrukin, known today as Khorsabad. The palace, on a high platform, had many courtyards and rooms which were lavishly decorated with frescoes and carvings.

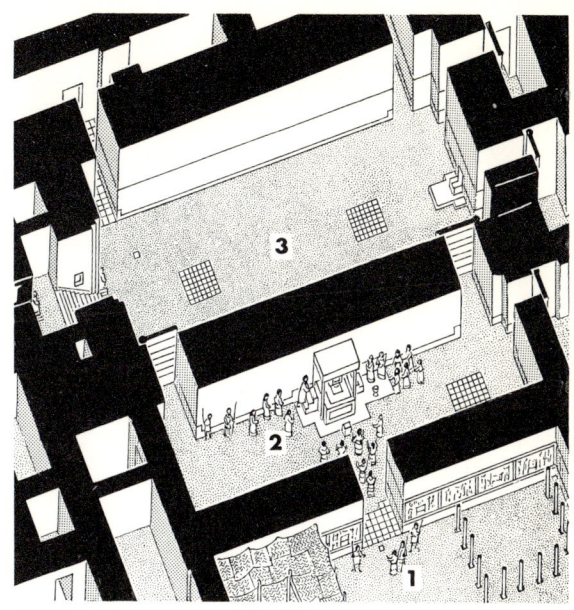

MARI, Open court (1), Throne Room (2) and Great Hall (3) in the Palace of Zimrilim, c. 1790 B.C.

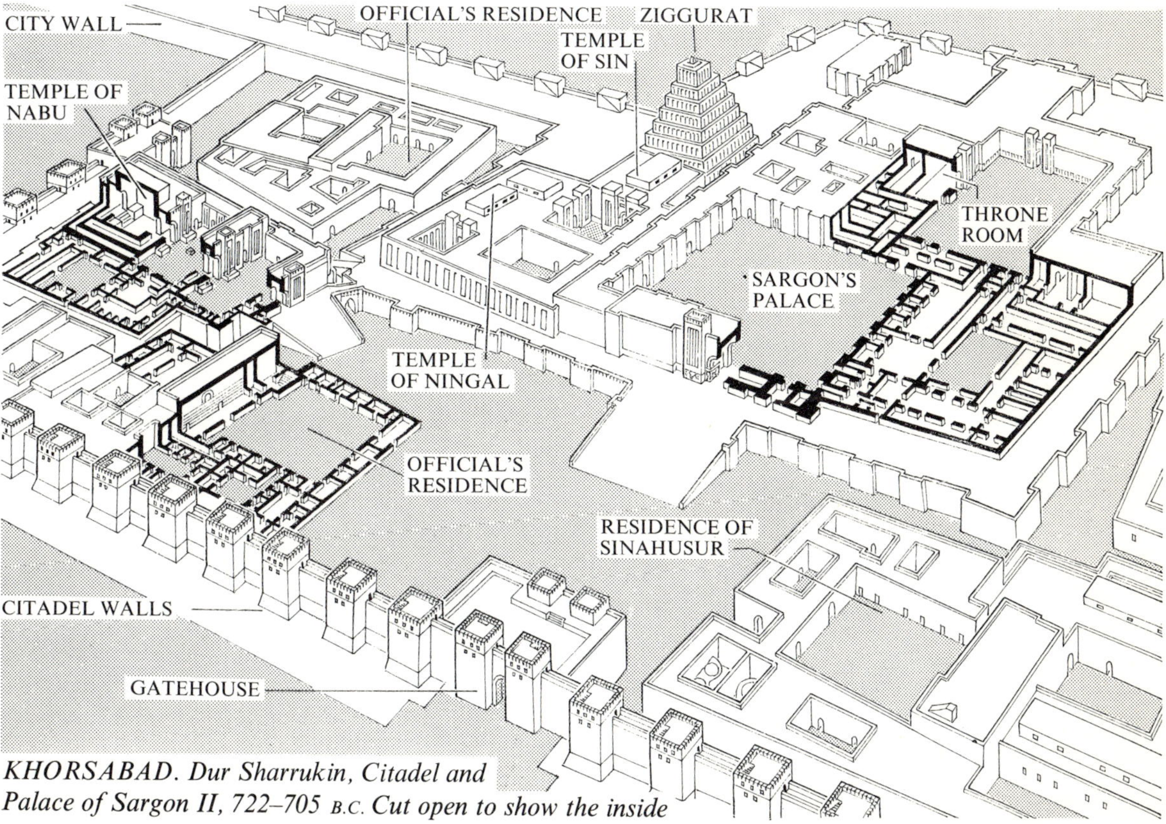

KHORSABAD. Dur Sharrukin, Citadel and Palace of Sargon II, 722–705 B.C. *Cut open to show the inside*

19

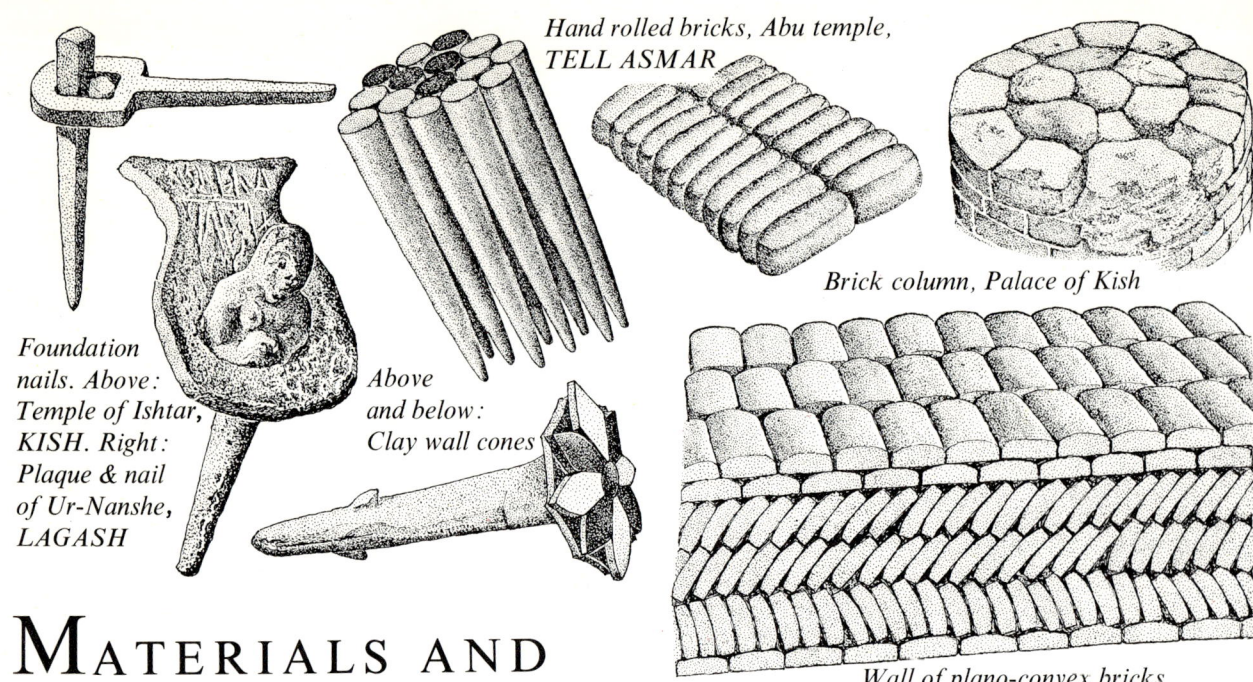

Hand rolled bricks, Abu temple, TELL ASMAR

Foundation nails. Above: Temple of Ishtar, KISH. Right: Plaque & nail of Ur-Nanshe, LAGASH

Above and below: Clay wall cones

Brick column, Palace of Kish

Wall of plano-convex bricks

Materials and Construction

The basic material for building was mud. It was made up into bricks varying in colour from red to grey and black, depending from where the clay had been taken. First the ground was dug over to let water from the river or nearby canal seep in; then straw or sometimes sand was added and the whole area trodden over, either by men or animals. Lumps of the prepared material were dug out and the brickmaker took a sufficient quantity to make one brick; he thumped it and rolled it on the ground into an oblong shape which was then allowed to dry in the sun. A later method was to press the clay into a wooden frame. The Sumerians did not level off the clay, but left some above the edge of the frame; this was then lifted off and the brick was left to dry in the sun, or, if it needed to be waterproofed, it was baked hard in a kiln. These bricks were called plano-convex. They were either laid flat with the curved side uppermost, or set on edge in a herringbone pattern (see above). Sundried bricks were bonded together with mud

20

Left: Well head in the Gimilsin temple TELL ASMAR
Above: Vaults in palace store-room DUR KURIGALZU

mortar, which was pushed into place with the hands. In later times the surface of bricks was squared off. Each brickmaker had his own mould; some were specially shaped to produce the bricks which were needed for columns, or arches; the latter being built over timber centering. To prevent erosion wall cones were used, sometimes in decorative bands (pages 4–5), or in an all-over pattern (pages 8–9); mud plaster was also applied.

Stone was very little used in the south of the country, but in the north in Assyrian times it was employed for decoration (pages 16–17). Stone was carried on the river on rafts which were supported on inflated skins, or on boats which were then dragged to the site by teams of men who pulled them over wooden rollers. The stones were roughly cut to shape before they were transported, as the builders did not want to move more weight than was necessary.

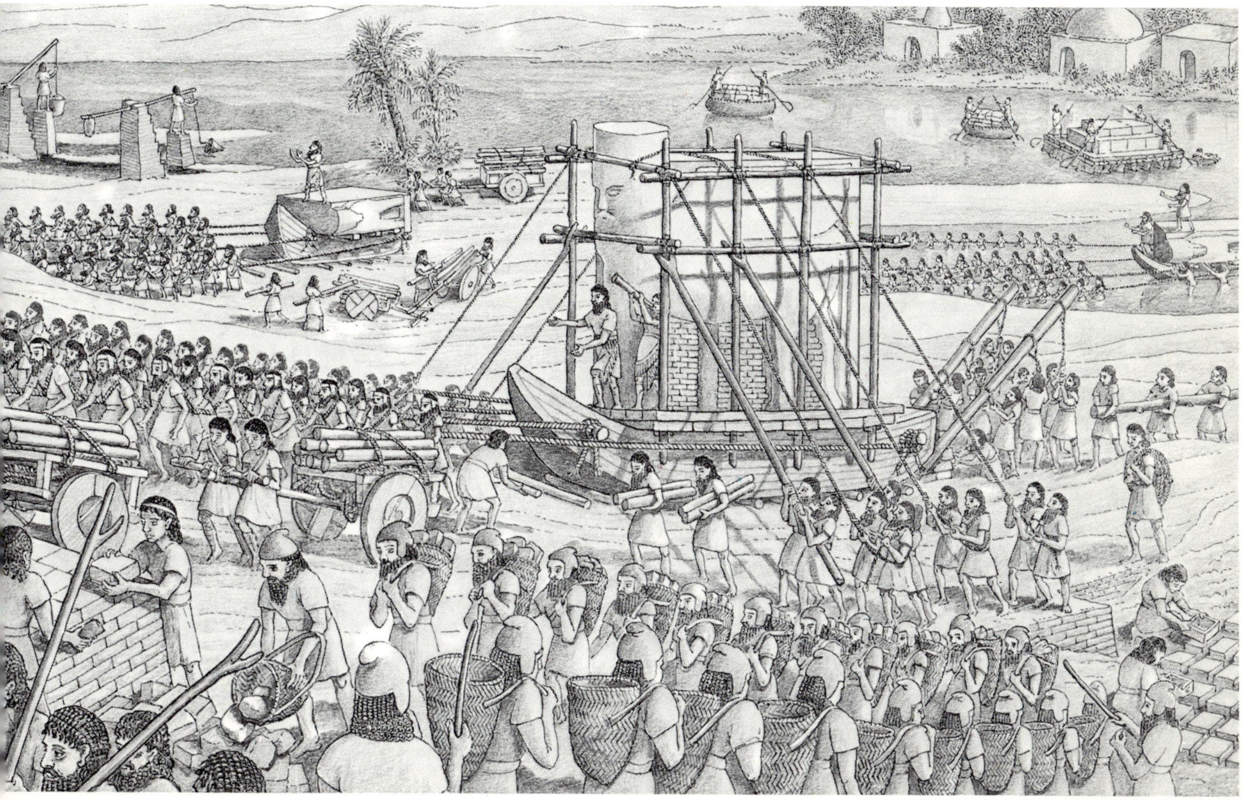

MARI. *Bathroom and latrine of the Governor of the Palace*

At Mari, water for the baths, which stood on a baked-brick platform covered with bitumen, was heated on a brazier placed under a chimney-hood in the corner of the room. The lavatory, of the 'squatter' type still used in eastern countries, had two steps of bitumened baked brick with a drain between them; interlocking terracotta pipes underneath took the waste away to vaulted sewers.

Palace gates and doors were made of wood. As hinges were not used, each leaf was built on to a rounded pivot post – *harr* – which was fastened to the wall at the top by a ring; below ground-level a bronze shoe held the bottom of the post, which was rounded off so that it could turn in a depression cut in a stone. In an example at the palace of Balawat the doors were bound by horizontal bronze bands set at intervals across each leaf. These bands, carved in relief with battle scenes, were curved to fit round the pivot post. It has been noticed that the bands at the top were longer than those at the bottom, so allowing for the tapering of the *harr*.

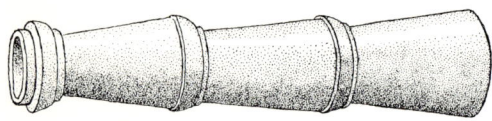 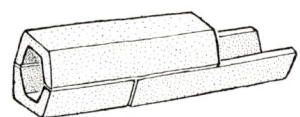 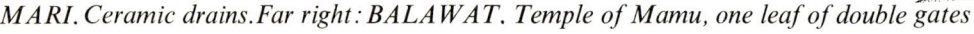

MARI. *Ceramic drains. Far right:* BALAWAT. *Temple of Mamu, one leaf of double gates*

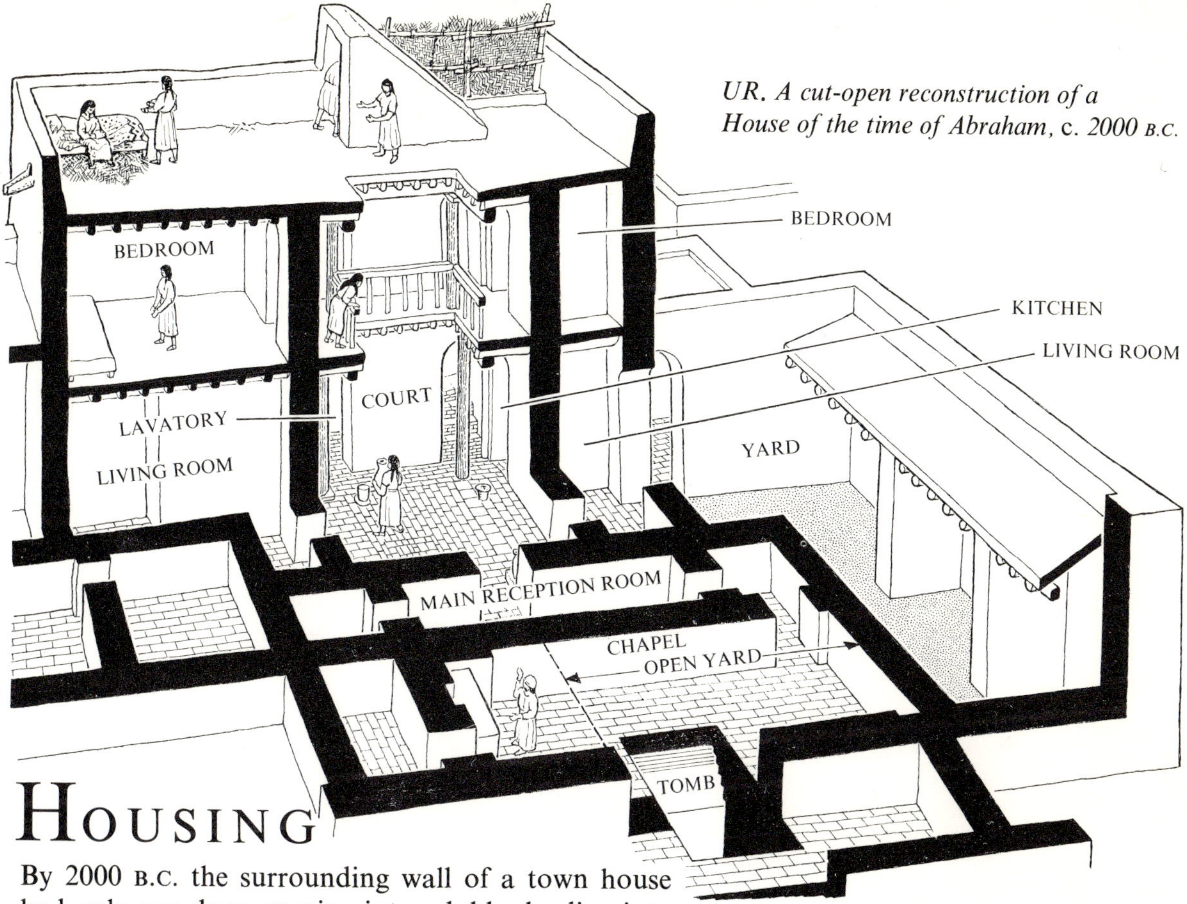

UR. A cut-open reconstruction of a House of the time of Abraham, c. 2000 B.C.

Housing

By 2000 B.C. the surrounding wall of a town house had only one door opening into a lobby leading into a courtyard. There were stands for water jars and a drain so that visitors could wash the dust from their feet. As there were no windows the long, narrow living-room had a wide door to admit light. In the kitchen there was a bread oven and a raised cooking hearth, as well as an open fireplace; brick benches may have been used as beds by the servants. In another house (right) a long room almost the width of the courtyard was used to receive guests with a further courtyard and the private quarters behind.

Some houses, such as that at Ur (above), had a chapel with a plastered and white washed mud-brick altar, before which offerings of food were made; behind it was a recess for burning incense. The household gods stood on a pillar decorated in imitation of wood panelling. The altar area had a penthouse type roof, but there was also an unroofed portion beneath which was the family burial vault.

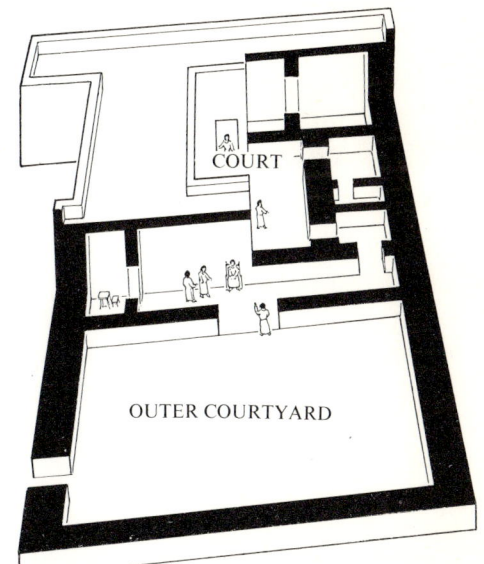

ASSUR. House cut open to show the inside

23

A ROYAL BURIAL AT UR. Graves were also found outside the city walls. These were rectangular pits in which the body was laid, either in a roll of matting fastened by a long copper pin, or in a wickerwork or wooden coffin. Tools, weapons and vessels containing food were placed near by.

It was beneath such graves that the earlier tombs of the god-kings of Ur, *c.* 3500 B.C., were found. These burials were very elaborate, as it was then the custom for the ruler's courtiers to die with him. The grave consisted of a great open pit which was approached by a sloping passageway. The tomb chamber, set in a corner of the pit, was built with walls of limestone and topped by a vaulted roof with semicircular ends which were corbelled: each brick course projecting beyond the one below it. Wooden beams spanning the tomb supported timbers on which earth and straw were laid to form the curve. This was covered with limestone or brick rubble laid in mortar,

finished with a plaster of lime cement.

Accompanied by two or three attendants, the body of the king was placed in the chamber with pots of food and drink set beside it; the door was then bricked up. The king's goods were taken into the pit in carts drawn by animals. Men and women dressed in finery and soldiers who were fully armed moved into their places; each had a small cup which apparently contained a drug which they drank. They then lay down in an orderly fashion to await death. Before earth was thrown into the pit, the animals which had been harnessed to the carts were killed. The pit was filled in until only the top of the tomb chamber showed; on this 'floor' a funeral feast was held at which a human sacrifice may have been offered. More earth was thrown in and further offerings made; this continued until the pit and passageway were full. At ground-level some kind of funerary chapel must have been erected to mark the burial.

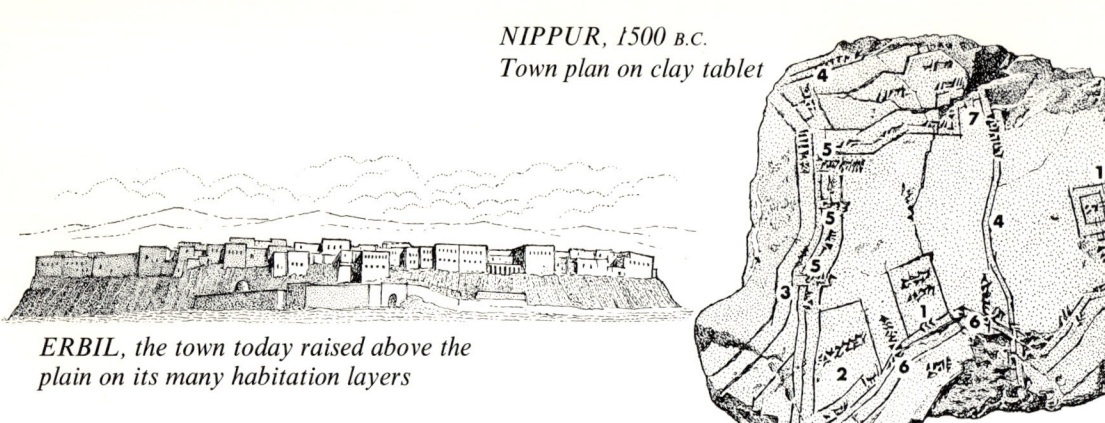

NIPPUR, 1500 B.C. Town plan on clay tablet

ERBIL, the town today raised above the plain on its many habitation layers

1: Temples. 2: Park. 3: Euphrates. 4: Canals. 5: Gates in S.W. wall. 6: Gates in S.E. wall. 7: Gate in N.W. wall.

Towns and Cities

In northern Mesopotamia the earliest people were farmers and cattle breeders, for the brown soil of the uplands was good for cultivation, and there was pasture land for the animals. A farm settlement of about 5000 B.C. has been found at Tell Hassuna. Lying on top of primitive pottery and tools were the remains of six layers of houses; the later ones each had six or seven rooms arranged in two blocks round a courtyard. The walls were of dried mud and the floors a mixture of clay and chopped straw. Great jars of unbaked clay had been sunk into the floor to store grain. At Arpachiyah the streets of the settlement had been cobbled, and this must have been the result of work undertaken by the whole community. From such communal undertakings, and in particular the building of shrines, it would seem that towns and cities developed. As the shrine developed into a large temple complex, the growth in trade resulting from the export of surplus offerings and gifts (page 5) meant an increase in the wealth and well-being of the community, which in turn expanded from a settlement into a city.

The fertile soil was deposited on the flat land between the rivers by the flooding which took place in early summer. However, after the flood it was too late to sow crops, and had they been sown beforehand the seedlings would have been washed out of the ground. So control of the waters was essential, and here again community effort was needed to build irrigation canals. The canals were dug out and their banks lined with bundles of reeds or matting to prevent the mud walls from being washed away. When the plants required water a hole could be opened in the bank and filled in when sufficient water had passed through. The channels needed constant dredging, and to make sure that there was a supply of reeds each town had a marsh patch. By 3000 B.C., there were many prosperous cities in the south of the country, resulting from the successful irrigation of the land.

UR. The central part of the city at the time of Abraham. 2100–1900 B.C. The house marked X may be seen in greater detail in the upper drawing on page 23

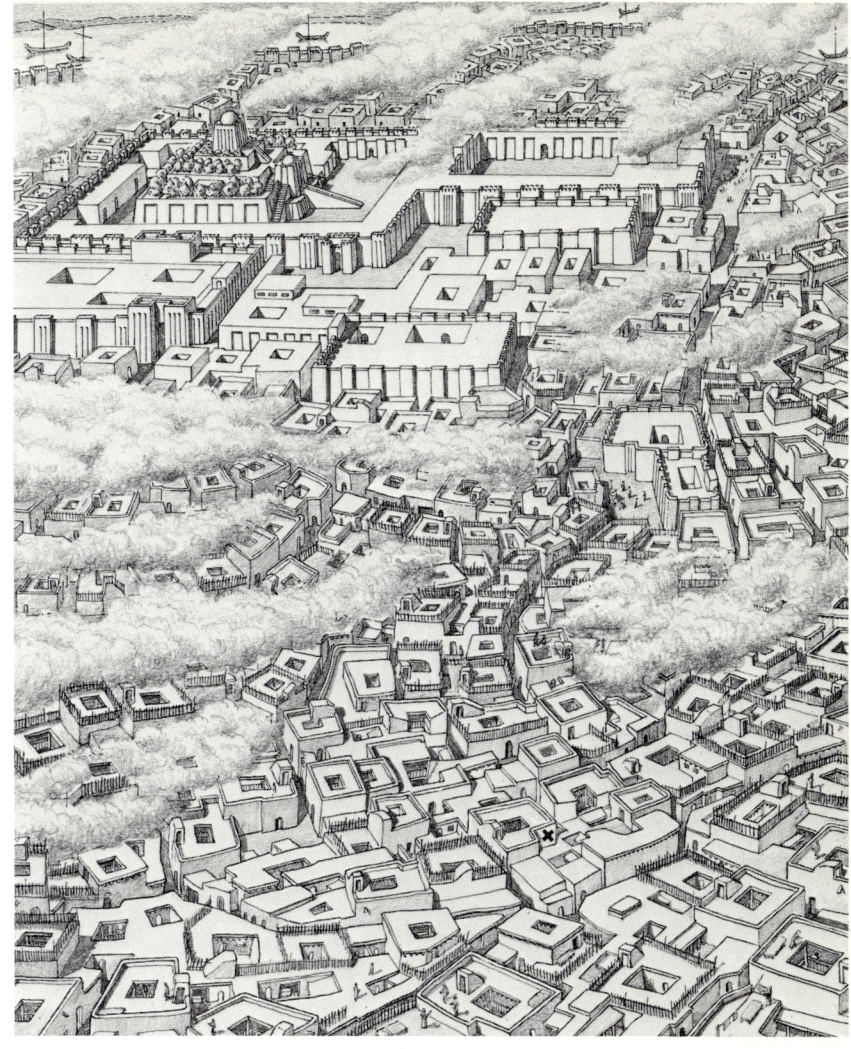

Each city had a wall around it for protection; before it was built the ground was marked out by the *Ensi* (page 4). Further protection was sometimes given by a moat and beyond this lay the fields and irrigation canals. When small settlements developed into towns, the people built their houses where they pleased as there was no overall planning. The result was towns with very narrow winding alleyways which made the movement of traffic and the disposal of rubbish very difficult. Sometimes the outer walls of corner houses were rounded instead of being square, to allow for movement in the road. The high outer walls threw shadows which gave some measure of protection from the sun. Only one doorway led from the street into the courtyard of each dwelling, where the householder could sit in the pleasant shade. At night he could enjoy the breeze on the flat roof of the house.

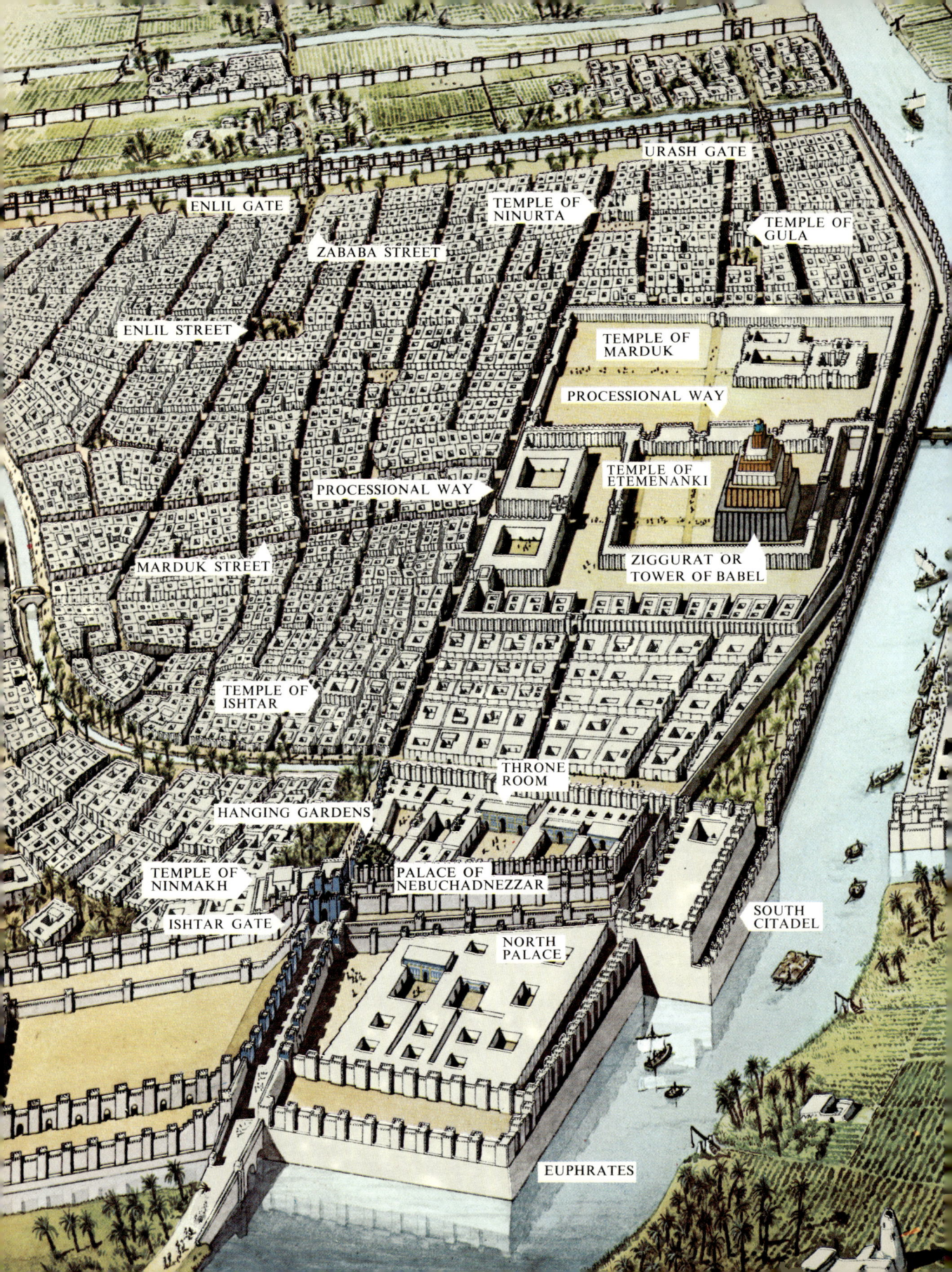

BABYLON
IN THE TIME OF NEBUCHADNEZZAR

By 612 B.C. the power of Assyria had fallen and Babylon had once more become the greatest power in the land under her kings Nabopolassar 626–605, and his son Nebuchadnezzar 605–562, who set about rebuilding in great splendour. The Euphrates, flowing from north to south, divided the city and was spanned by a bridge which had piers built of brick with battered walls which met at a point at the front and back to allow for the water currents. The Greek historian, Herodotus, writing in the 4th cent. B.C., says that the superstructure, which was of wood, was divided into sections which could be removed at night to prevent robbers entering the city.

There were eight gates in the walls which surrounded the city; the main entrance lay along the processional way and through the Ishtar Gate (pages 32–33). Just within this gate was the king's palace which was decorated with floral designs on glazed bricks; it had five courtyards, and a building, possibly the famous Hanging Gardens (frontispiece), which were probably terraces on which trees were planted. It is thought that Nebuchadnezzar built the gardens for his wife to remind her of her own country which was hilly.

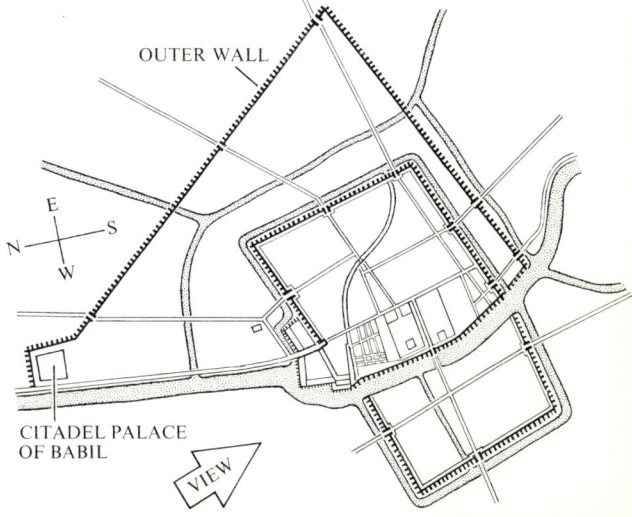

Education and the law

Attached to many of the temples and palaces of Sumer were schools, or 'Tablet Houses', where scribes were trained to run both temple and city administration. The main part of a scribe's training consisted of learning cuneiform. Most pupils were sons of wealthy, important men; this is known because at the bottom of each piece of his work the pupil had to inscribe his name and also the profession of his father.

During excavations at Mari a room was found which must have been a school room of the 'Tablet House'. The walls were mud-plastered and the floor paved with tiles of burnt brick. Benches were set in rows down the length of the room and round the walls. Placed on the floor between the benches were large basins to hold clay. Each pupil took a quantity of the clay and kneaded and formed it into a cushion-shaped tablet upon which he wrote his exercises; these consisted of careful copying of a tablet which the master had written as an example.

The headmaster, called the 'School Father', was assisted by other teachers and monitors, including 'Big Brother with the stick', who attended to pupils – 'Sons of the Tablet House' – who were careless and slow in their work, or

THE PALACE, MARI, c. 1780 B.C. *The schoolroom or tablet house*

late for school! Many school tablets have been found in the ancient city of Shuruppak. One tablet described the school day in the form of questions and answers. The teacher asked where the boy went in the morning; the boy answered, 'I went to school'. He was asked if he played about on the way and what lessons he had to do. He replied that he had to write his homework, then prepare a new tablet on which he copied a text. He ate the lunch which his mother had given to him, and was then questioned about his work by the 'School Father'. After a further written task he went home, where he repeated his lessons to his own father. The writing on the tablets shows that not all days were so good. When he was caught talking in class he was caned, and again when he left school without permission. When he told his father what had happened to him, the headmaster was invited to dine and given gifts! Many copies of this composition were found, so it must have been a favourite exercise of the teachers.

By about 2500 B.C., not only pupils were at the schools but also scholars, mathematicians, scientists, geographers and lawyers. The lawyers wrote down the laws which governed the lives of the people. These laws, the results of decisions by rulers such as Lippit-Ishtar, Eshnunna and Ur-Nammu, were gathered together for future reference. The most famous set of laws is the Code of Hammurabi, which was found on a pillar – stele –

Code of Hammurabi on a black basalt stele, circa 18th C. B.C.

EL OBEID, Temple of Ninhursag limestone foundation tablet, c. 2600 B.C.

of black stone. The stele, now in the Louvre in Paris, shows the king standing before the sun-god and god of justice, Shamash; columns of cuneiform list laws which it was believed the king received from the god. They dealt with daily life and trade; for example, if an architect built a house for a freeman and it collapsed and killed the householder, then the architect could be put to death; or if a slave was killed the architect had to provide the owner with a new one.

As king, Hammurabi was responsible for the digging and repairing of the canals around Babylon which were essential to the life of the people. The stele records that a man had to keep the dykes and banks of the canals which ran through his land in good order. If he did not and his neighbour suffered inconvenience, he must provide him with grain to make good his loss. The law also laid down that every man in the kingdom must work on the digging of new, or repairing of old, canals.

THE ISHTAR GATE, BABYLON, spanned the great processional way built for the god Marduk, whose statue, carried in a boat, had to be taken outside the city for religious purposes at certain times of the year. The road which had been over-built several times consisted of bricks covered with asphalt which served as a base for a flagged pavement: white limestone down the centre and red breccia at the sides. On the bevelled edges of the stones were inscriptions saying the road had been built by Nebuchadnezzar. On either side were high walls faced with blue enamelled bricks decorated in low relief with rows of lions, the symbol of Ishtar. A model of the animal must first have been constructed from which a mould for each brick was made. After moulding, the bricks were burnt and then the contours were outlined in black and infilled with coloured liquid enamel. After a further firing the enamel set and the lines mixed with the colours. Each brick had marks

32

on its sides which corresponded with marks on those adjoining it so the pattern fitted.

The gateway was of the standard pattern with two tower blocks and an enclosed courtyard. It could be closed at each end by pairs of great wooden leafed doors. The brickwork was again enamelled in blue, and rising up each tower were alternate rows of brightly enamelled bulls and dragons – *sirrush*. These creatures were placed there to frighten off evil spirits and protect the city.

The builders of Babylon showed their skill by the way they made use of expansion joints. Not all the walls were built on foundations of the same depth; there was, therefore, a danger that parts of the structure might sink to different levels, which would have meant that the walls would crack. To counteract this, a narrow vertical space was left between adjoining walls to allow for movement. Modern builders leave a similar expansion joint when building with concrete.

The Biblical city of Ashtaroth in Syria, from the Palace of Tiglath-Pileser III, NIMRUD

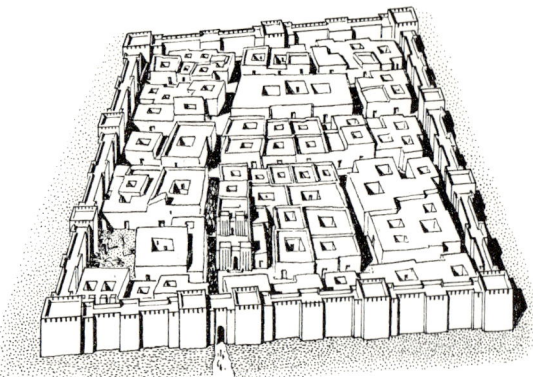

SHADUPPUM, Fortified administrative area of an agricultural district, c. 2000 B.C. (Shaduppum is in the boundaries of Baghdad)

Fortifications

In the excavations of the ancient city of Nippur archaeologists discovered many thousands of clay tablets, among which was one showing a map of the city at about 1500 B.C. (page 26). Although the scribe marked in the main buildings and canals, it was the walls and gates in which he seemed to be especially interested; as a result, it has been suggested that the map was prepared for defence purposes against attacks by enemies.

The story of Mesopotamia was one of struggle. Many times power changed hands, and from very early times cities were surrounded by walls which gave protection, and also showed their importance and strength. It was the duty of the ruler to pull down the walls of cities that he conquered, and to keep those of his own domain in good repair. The double walls of the city of Warka, built about 3500 B.C. of plano-convex bricks (page 20), were strengthened with semicircular bastions.

From Assyrian reliefs it is possible to learn much about the fortifications of later cities. In the illustration of Ashtaroth the city is seen standing on a hill surrounded by a double wall with towers topped with crenellations, through which the archers could shoot at the enemy on the ground below.

Sometimes schemes for fortifications were so vast that they were never finished. At Nineveh, for example, the capital city of the Assyrian Empire during the reign of Sennacherib, 704–681 B.C., the outer walls were left incomplete. A second set of walls surrounded an inner citadel which contained the palace, government quarters and temples.

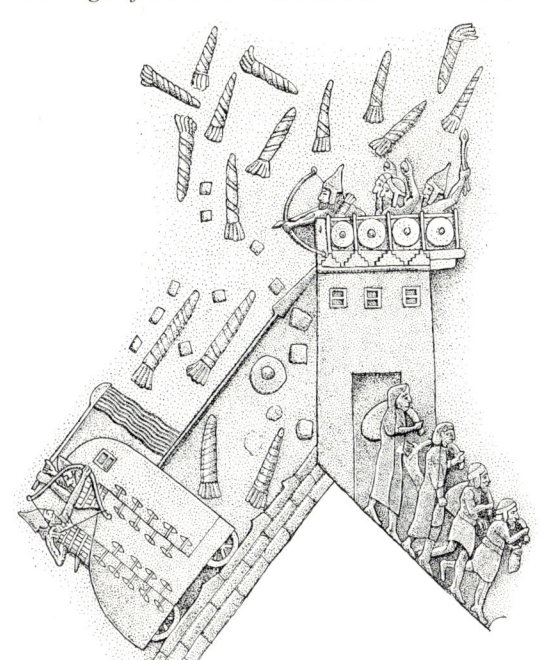

NINEVEH, Palace of Sennacherib, 704–681 B.C.
The siege of Lachish in S. Palestine in 700 B.C.

NINEVEH, Palace of Assurbanipal, 668–627 B.C.
The siege and destruction of Hamanu in Elam

The city of Khorsabad – Dur Sharrukin – was strongly fortified with two sets of walls built on foundations of rough undressed stone laid directly on the ground. In place of mortar, layers of reed matting were used at intervals to act as binders, in the same way that they were used in the *ziggurats* (pages 12–13). The walls were battered at the base on the outside, but were vertical on the inside. Both faces were coated with white plaster, and they were further strengthened by towers which provided good defensive positions from which archers could protect the base of the walls between. The main gateway also had towers and the outer gate was lined on either side with human-headed winged bulls – *lamassus*. These *lamassus* – sometimes bulls and sometimes lions – always had five legs so that, whether viewed from the front or from the side, they would appear to have the right number of legs (see cover).

The outer walls of Babylon (pages 28–29) had two faces of burnt brick with rubble infilling. The top of the walls was wide enough to take two chariots abreast, each with four horses. The parapet with its stepped crenellations was from one to two feet thick and six feet high. In addition to these fortifications, Nebuchadnezzar protected his kingdom by erecting the great Median Wall, which ran from the Tigris to the Euphrates, some fifty miles north of Babylon.

35

THE SIEGE OF HAMANU was depicted on the reliefs on the walls of the north palace of Assurbanipal, 688–672 B.C., in Nineveh. The Assyrian army brought up many war machines in their efforts to take the city. Soldiers excavated under the walls, shoring up the hole with timber which they then set on fire so that the brickwork would collapse. They wheeled high wooden towers, protected by a covering of skins, close to the walls. Archers stood on a platform and attacked the defenders on the parapets. Wooden battering rams, tipped with iron, were covered with a timber and leather structure to protect the men who swung the ram backwards and forwards to make a breach. Water was poured over the outside to prevent the machine being set on fire. The defenders tried to catch the ram with chains or ropes and overturn it. They loosed arrows and threw boiling oil, stones and flaming torches on the attackers.

The soldiers wore metal helmets or close

fitting skull-caps with cheek-pieces. They had breastplates reinforced with metal, and high boots laced at the front. Some archers were protected by shields made of bundles of plaited reeds, with a curved top covered with leather; these shields were so big that they had to be carried by another man. Horsemen carried lances, short daggers, and small shields. Charioteers had bows and arrows.

When a city was taken it was plundered of all its treasures. The walls and buildings were destroyed and the inhabitants lined up before the city gate where the conqueror's throne was set up. The king and nobles were tortured and burnt alive or impaled on stakes; the men were taken into slavery for such heavy tasks as moving the great stone *lamassus* (page 21). Artists and craftsmen were pressed into the king's service, while the rest of the population was removed to distant parts. The victorious army celebrated and made sacrifices to the gods.

URUK, Innin Temple, Water God from the dado of baked bricks: see the drawing at the top of page 15

From the map it can be seen that the lives of the people were dominated by the land in which they lived. The Sumerians in the flat lands of the south, flourished from about 4000 to 2000 B.C., living in city-states, the earliest being Eridu near to the Persian Gulf. The ancient legend of the creation says that 'All the lands were sea, then Eridu was made'. Other important cities were Uruk (Warka, Erech), Kish and Ur. Babylon was the dominant power from 1894 to 1595 B.C., but she was overthrown by the Assyrians from the mountainous regions of the north. These people conquered all the surrounding lands and established a great empire; this in its turn was overthrown, and its cities buried in the dust.

The last era of greatness in the Land of the Two Rivers was that of the Neo – new – Babylonian period under Nebuchadnezzar. Slowly the people lost their independence, conquered by Persians, then Greeks and lastly Parthians. Although the cities were still occupied many of the inhabitants were settlers from outside. The old gods were replaced by foreign deities, and the civilization, which gave the ancient world scholars, writing, literature, mathematics and science, fell into decay and died.

ACKNOWLEDGEMENTS

The authors wish to thank Professor R. A. Crossland, for the loan of material, and Professor Seton Lloyd, and the staff of the Department of Western Asiatic Antiquities of the British Museum, for comment and advice given during the preparation of this book. In addition they acknowledge their indebtedness to the following authors: Andrae, W.; *Das Wiedererstandene Assur*, Leipzig, 1938; Baqir, T. *Excavations at Aqar Quf*, Iraq, Supp. 1944/45; Barnett, R. D. *Assyrian Palace Reliefs in the British Museum*, London, 1970; Barnett, R. D., and Wiseman, D. J. *Fifty Masterpieces of Ancient Near Eastern Art*, London, 1969; Baumann, H. *The Land of Ur*, London, 1969; Beek, M.A. *Atlas of Mesopotamia*, London, 1962; Contenau, G. *Everyday Life in Babylon and Assyria*, London, 1954; Delougaz, P. I. *Plano-Convex Bricks*, O.I.C., 20, Chicago, 1933; *The Temple Oval at Khafeje*, Chicago, 1940; Frankfort, H. *The Art and Architecture of the Ancient Orient*, Harmondsworth, 1956; *Ishchali*, O.I.C., Comm. 20, Chicago, 1936; *The Birth of Civilization in the Near East*, New York, 1956; Frankfort, Lloyd and Jacobsen, *The Gimilsin Temple and the Palace of the Rulers at Tell Asmar*, O.I.P., vol XLIII, Illinois, 1940; Hodges, H. *Technology in the Ancient World*, Harmondsworth, 1971; *Dur Kurigalzu*, Iraq, Supp. 1945; Jacobsen, T. *Primitive Democracy in Ancient Mesopotamia*, Journal of Near Eastern Studies, vol 2, no. 3, Chicago, 1943; Jaward, A. J. *The Advent of the Era of Townships in Northern Mesopotamia*, Leiden, 1965; Koldwey, R. *Excavations at Babylon*, London, 1914; Kramer, S. *History Begins at Sumer*, London, 1956; Lampl, P. *Cities and Planning in the Ancient Near East*, London, 1968; Langdon, S. *Kish*, vol I, Paris, 1924; Layard, A. H. *Nineveh and Its Remains*, vols 1 and 2, London, 1854; *Monuments of Nineveh*, London, 1853; Lenzen, H. J. *Uruk-Warka, Die Entwicklung der Zikkurat*, Leipzig, 1941; Lloyd, S. *Sumer*, vols 3, 4, Baghdad, 1947, 1948; *Tell Uqair*, Journal of Near Eastern Studies, vol 2, Chicago, 1942; *The Art of the Ancient Near East*, London, 1961; Loud, G. and Altman C. H. B. *Khorsabad* vols 1, 2, Chicago, 1936, 1938; Loud, Frankfort and Jacobsen, *Khorsabad*, O.I.P., vol XXXVIII, Chicago, 1936; Mackay, E. *A Sumerian Palace at Kish*, Field Museum of Natural History, Anthropology Memoirs, vol. 1, no. 2, Chicago, 1929; Mallowan, M. E. I. *Early Mesopotamia and Iran*, London, 1965; Moortgat, A. *The Art of Ancient Mesopotamia*, London, 1969; Oppenheim, A. L. *Ancient Mesopotamia*, Chicago, 1964; Parrot, A. *Mission Archéologique de Mari*, vols 1 and 2, Paris, 1956–59; Roux, G. *Ancient Iraq*, Harmondsworth, 1966; Speiser, E. A. *Excavations at Tepe Gawra*, vol I, Philadelphia, 1935; Stearns, J. B. *Reliefs from the Palace of Ashurnasirpal II*, Archiv Für Orientforschung, Supp. 15, Berlin, 1961; Wetzel, F. *Assur und Babylon*, Berlin, 1949; Wetzel, F. and Weissbach F. H. *Babylon. Esagila und Etemenanki*, vol VII, Ausgrabungen der Deutschen Orient-Gesellschaft, Osnabruck, 1967; Woolley, C. L. *Ur Excavations*, vols 2 and 5, London, 1934, 1939.

ABBREVIATIONS: O.I.C., Oriental Institute of University of Chicago. O.I.P. Oriental Institute of University of Philadelphia.

INDEX

Altar 7, 9, 10, 18, 23
Arpachiya 26, 39
Assur 15, 39
Assurbanipal 2, 36
Assurnasirpal II 16–17
Assyrian 16–17, 21, 29, 34–8

Babylon 1, 14–15, 28–33, 35, 38–9
Balawat 22, 39
Bath 22
Bench 23, 30
Bitumen 6, 7, 12–14, 22
Boat 21, 28
Brick 4, 7, 8, 10–14, 15, 17–18, 20–5, 29, 30, 32–3, 35, 38
Bridge 28–9

Canal 2, 26, 28, 31, 34
Carving 2, 3, 16–17, 19, 22, 35
Chapel 7, 18, 23, 25
Clay 3, 8, 15, 20, 26, 30–1, 34
Column 8–10, 21
Cone 4, 5, 7–9, 20–1
Courtyard 10–11, 14–15, 17–19, 23, 26, 28–9, 33
Cuneiform 5, 30–1

Door 2, 22–3, 25, 33
Drain 6, 22–3
Dur Kurigalzu 21

El Obeid 2, 8, 31, 39
Enamel 32–3
Erbil 26, 39
Eridu 7, 38–9
Eshnunna 18, 31, 39
Euphrates 2, 26, 28–9, 35, 39

Fortification 27, 34–7
Foundation nail 11, 20
Frescoes 16–17, 19

Garden 1, 28–9
Gate 22, 28–9, 32–5
Gateway 14–15, 18–19, 26, 32, 34–5
Gods 4, 6, 9–11, 14–15, 18–19, 23–4, 28–9, 31–3, 38

Hall 8, 9, 18–19
Hammurabi 14, 31
Hearth 7, 9, 23
House 2, 3, 6, 23, 26–8

Ishchali 14, 39
Ishtar 14, 28–9, 32–3

Khafajah 2, 10-11, 39
Khorsabad 19, 35, 39
Khurdistan 2, 15–16, 39
Kish 18, 20, 38–9

Lagash 14, 20, 39
Law 30–1

Mari 3, 14, 19, 22, 30, 39
Mortar 21, 24, 35
Mosaic 8, 33
Mountain 2, 7, 16
Mudbrick 6, 7, 9–10, 16, 19, 20

Nebuchadnezzar 28–9, 32, 35, 38
Nimrud 16, 34, 39
Nineveh 2, 3, 34–6, 39
Nippur 26, 34, 39

Painting 7, 13, 16–17, 19
Palace 2, 16–19, 21–2, 28–30, 35
Plano-convex 10, 20–1
Plaster 16–17, 19, 21, 23, 25, 30, 35

Reeds 2, 3, 7, 13, 24, 26, 35
Roof 7, 17, 23–4

Sanctuary 10, 14, 18
Sargon II 19
Schoolroom 30
Seal 3, 4, 6
Sennacherib 34–5
Shrine 6, 9–11, 13–15
Stone 7, 16–17, 19, 21, 24, 32, 35
Sumer 6, 7, 9, 14–15, 20, 30, 38–9

Tablet 3, 26, 30–1
Tell Asmar 10, 18, 20–1, 39
Tell Brak 39
Tell Uqair 6, 39
Temple 2, 4–11, 14–15, 18–19, 26–8, 30–1, 34, 38
Tent 3
Tepe Gawra 4–6, 39
Throne room 16–19
Tigris 2, 14, 16, 26, 35, 39
Timber 17, 19, 21–2, 24, 29, 34, 36
Tomb 12, 23, 24–5
Tower 12, 14, 19, 32, 34–7
Town 26–7, 34
Tree 11, 13

Ur 11, 13–15, 23–5, 27, 31, 38–9
Uruk see Warka

Wall 7, 12, 15–17, 19–20, 23–4, 26–8, 32–7
Warka 2, 7–9, 15, 34, 38–9
Well 21

Ziggurat 1, 7, 11–13, 19, 27–8, 35

For a comparative Time Chart of the buildings of Mesopotamia with those of other early civilisations, see *The Buildings of Ancient Man*, page 39

---

*First published 1974 jointly by
Brockhampton Press Ltd, Leicester and
Young Scott Books,
Addison-Wesley Publishing Company, Inc.,
Reading Massachusetts 01867, USA.*

*UK ISBN 0 340 16425 5
USA ISBN 0-201-09447-9*

All rights reserved. No part of this publication may be reproduced or transmitted in any form or by any means, electronic or mechanical, including photocopy recording, or any information storage and retrieval system, without permission in writing from the publisher.

Library of Congress Cataloguing in Publication Data

Leacroft, Helen
The buildings of ancient Mesopotamia

Summary: Describes the palaces, temples, and houses of Mesopotamia, including Ur, Babylonia, Sumer, and Assyria, as they must have been according to the evidence unearthed by archaeologists.
1. Architecture—Mesopotamia—Juvenile literature.
2. Mesopotamia—Civilization—Juvenile literature.
(1. Architecture—Mesopotamia. 2. Mesopotamia—Civilization)
I. Leacroft, Richard, joint author. II. Title.
NA220.L42   722'.51   73-22559
ISBN 0-201-09447-9

Printed in Great Britain by Jarrold & Sons Ltd, Norwich